THE SUCCESS OF PRIVATE LABELS

WAKE UP CALL FOR TRADITIONAL BRANDS!

CYNTHIA ZACLIS RABINOVITZ

THE SUCCESS OF PRIVATE LABELS

WAKE UP CALL FOR TRADITIONAL BRANDS!

NAVEGAR EDITORA

NAVEGAR EDITORA

Comercial Editora Hermano & Bugelli Ltda.
MF - Navegar Editora
Rua Belém, 93 - Belenzinho
Cep 03057-010 - São Paulo - SP
Phone: (5511) 6096-8530
Fax: (5511) 6096-8530
Internet: www.navegareditora.com.br
E-mail: www.navegareditora@superig.com.br

Copyeditor: Rubenal Hermano
Editorial Project: Rubenal Hermano
Originals Development: Angela Bugelli
Edition and Diagramation: VB Santos S/C Ltda.
Cover: Leonardo Hermano
Proofreader: The author

Printed in Brazil 2004

To my son, Eduardo
To my husband, Ury
To my parents, Denise and Lionel
To my sister, Shelly

You are everything!

I LOVE YOU!
THANKS!

TABLE OF CONTENTS

Introduction..11

PART I:

Private Labels..15
Propitious Landscape..21
Specific Categories of Private Labels..24
Private Labels as Real Brands..28

PART II:

Branding - Building Brands..33
The History of Branding..33
The Concept of Brand..34
Brands and Perceived Quality..35
Consumer Satisfaction and Branding..36
Brand Identity..36
Brand Equity..37
Brand and Consumer: Strong Relationship..37
Brand Personality..39
Brand Loyalty..40
Understanding Brand Loyalty - Crucial for Brands..43
Loyalty as a Strategic Issue..44
Private Labels as competitors..45

PART III:

New Branding Approach..49
Conclusion..61
References..62

PREFACE

The first part of the book presents the private labels, their history and evolution since the introduction up to development and success. The second part enters into the universe of the traditional brands, approaching issues related to branding such as origin of the term, general concept, perceived quality, consumer satisfaction, brand identity, brand equity, the relationship between the brand and the consumer, brand personality, and brand loyalty. The third part of the book discusses the national brands' challenges due to private label's success and also provides some suggestions for them. Finally, a conclusion section wraps up the analysis of the book, pointing that in order to face the new competitive retailer environment, fight against private labels and win the battle, national brands are expected to think about branding issues in a totally new way.

INTRODUCTION

Although some marketing executives did not believe that private labels would grow and succeed in the United States, American retail channels are providing more and more private labels for several product categories and their sales have been increasing lately. Private labels, also called house brands or store brands, are retailer's own brands offered at a lower price than national brands. Their retailer margins are usually twenty to thirty percent higher than national brands due to their lower development and production costs.

As McAlister and Kahn (1997) point out, it is very important to differentiate private labels from generic brands. Generic brands usually have no name, are offered in a black-and-white packaging and do not represent a strong menace to national brands due to their lower quality and inferior packaging. On the other hand, private labels represent a significant menace to national and traditional brands due to their continuous success as well as to their better quality, packaging and innovation.

Robert Tobin, president of Ahold USA, says: "the promotion of the store as a brand is now more important than promoting the brand in the store." According to a survey conducted by Cannondale Associates, seventy five percent of supermarket owners consider private labels or store brands the most important direction for them in the next millennium. Private labels are retailers' resources to build store loyalty since every store can sell Campbell's brands, for example, but only H-E-B can sell Hill Country Fare or Creamy Creations, two of their private lines of products.

Private labels are growing very fast, not only regarding consumer acceptance but also regarding the number of brands offered. According to Dunne, D. & Narasimhan, C. (1999), private labels are no longer considered as category killers, "me-too brands" or low-quality products. This growth represents a serious challenge for national brands. Cuneo, A. Z. (1999) points out in her article entitled "Retailtainment" that retail chains are expanding their private labels and backing their brands. In addition to that, consumers are becoming less loyal to brands and more sensitive to prices in a general sense.

According to Radice, C. (1998), industry sources believe that the growth of private labels will continue during the next years. Due to their technological advancements and quality improvements, private labels will be able to continuously offer several other attributes besides the lower price and, thus compete against national brands. Given this trend, national brands must begin to consider private labels as significant competitors and thus review their marketing strategy in order to win the battle.

Part 1

PRIVATE LABELS

Some people attribute the enormous growth of private labels in the United States to the recession of the early 90s, when consumers had less money to spend on groceries. However, private labels increased a lot during the good economic years as well. According to a study conducted by Gallup in 1996 with 1003 consumers over the age of 18 who were the household's primary shopper, ninety percent of the consumers were aware of private labels and eighty percent bought them often. Among the sampling, only sixty percent considered the price as the most important issue when they were buying private labels. Not only private labels are growing in units and expanding in categories but they are also increasing in consumer acceptance. According to Information Resources, consumers saved US$15.8 billion by choosing private labels over national brands (Murray, R. 1999). According to Phil Fitzell, a nationally private label expert, there are five important reasons for the enormous success of private labels lately.

1. Packaging or "Shelf-Look" Revolution

First of all, private labels have been facing a packaging or "shelf-look" revolution. Private labels' packaging are becoming as good and appealing as national brand's and sometimes their formats, colors and design are even better than national brands'. According to the Gallup study, seventy percent of the consumers believe private labels are packaged as well as national brands. Mark Smith, senior vice president at Marketing Management., Inc., a Fort Worth, Texas-based sales and marketing broker specializing in private labels, says: They (retailers) want things that add value to the store brand that might not exist on the branded side. Retailers are driving a level of sophistication in private label manufacturing because they are paying more attention to the profit attention of private label. They also see private label as a tool for customer loyalty because the same name can be on products wall to wall as is on the front of the store.

2. Better Quality

The second reason explaining the significant growth is that private labels are offering much more quality at a continuous lower price. The quality of private labels is also equal to national brands or even better in some categories. Nowadays, consumers no longer consider private labels low-quality products. According to the same study conducted by Gallup in 1996, eighty six percent of consumers consider private labels' quality equal or superior to national brands. This is not surprising since several important national brands' manufacturers such as Nestle, Campbell, Kraft, Phillip Morris and Hershey are beginning to produce private labels. There are positive arguments that provide incentives for manufacturers to produce private labels such as: excess capacity, economy of scale, relationship, and the fact that if they don't, their competitors will.

The better the quality of a private label, the more consumers will choose a private label product versus a national brand. Murray, R. (1999) says that among all product sales in the United States, twenty percent are private labels. According to a survey conducted by Cox Direct, eighty percent of the consumers buy a product in the store because of the price and the good value. The quality of private labels have been improving lately and today they can be compared to national brands, especially regarding categories with little product innovation.

Some retailers are going further regarding the quality issue, developing premium private labels brands such as H-E-B with its Personal Expression, Safeway's Bell-air, Town House and Lucern brands and Loblaw's President's Choice line of 1,500 items, including the leading chocolate cookie sold in Canada. Brian Sharoff, president of the Private Label Manufacturers Association, New York, said that "over the past ten years, with the introduction of premium private labels, many retailers realize they can go up as well as down by adding new tiers. Retailers feel as though they are upholding the single private label concepts with an extra tier at the top and value brands at the bottom for convenience."

3. Licensing Programs

The third reason is that licensing programs for private labels are expanding. This leads to a greater number of competitors and competition instigates better quality. Better quality causes consumers to buy more, which contributes to the success of private labels' sales.

4. One Product leads to the Entire Line

Fourth, when consumers accept one private label's product, they are usually very likely to accept the entire line of private labels. Wal-Mart, for example, launched their private label of Sam's American Choice for food and beverage and after six months this private label became Wal-Mart's largest selling brand according to Murray, R. (1999). Based on the success of this brand, Wal-Mart launched the next private label called Great Value. Both Great Value and Sam's American Food represented more than 5,000 SKUs (stock-keeping units). Wal-Mart launched other private labels such as Better Homes and Garden brand for home furnishings, garden supplies and paint, and Popular Mechanics brand for hunting apparel. Wal-Mart became the most important private label vendor in the United States, selling US$10 billion, which is ten percent of their sales.

5. All over the World

The fifth reason is that private labels are expanding all over the world. If analyzing their growth globally, private labels grew steadily in many European countries during the 1980s. According to Kahn and McAlister (1997), even during the economically successful years under Mrs. Thatcher's government, private labels increased in the United Kingdom. One successful case in the United Kingdom was the Classic Cola, a private label made by Cott Corporation for Sainsburry supermarket. Classic Cola was launched in April 1994 at a price twenty eighty percent lower than Coca Cola's. Nowadays, the private label Classic Cola accounts for sixty five percent of the total cola's sales through Sainsburry's and for fifteen percent of the entire United Kingdom cola market.

According to Kahn and McAlister (1997), private labels represent thirty two percent of the British supermarket volume, twenty four percent in France and twenty five percent in Canada. The two authors say that the growth of private labels was greater in Europe and Canada than in the United States because concentrated national chains have always dominated the Canadian and European retail environment in the past while non-concentrated chains have dominated the American retail environment. The top five British and French retail chains have represented sixty two percent and sixty five percent of sales, respectively. In Canada, Loblaws has controlled twenty seven percent of the grocery business alone. On the other hand, in the United States, not only were chains not very concentrated, but also the majority of them were regional and mid-sized. The top five American chains have represented only twenty percent of the overall grocery business.

Moreover, national brands in Europe and Canada have been fewer and their attributes such as sizes, packaging and flavors have not been as well developed as they have been in the United States. In addition to that, the United States' huge market size allows the country for greater economies of scale for advertising and production of national brands. This means that the competition among manufacturers of national brands in the United States has been stronger and the retail chains have been individually weaker than in England, Canada and France.

However, as it will be addressed later in this book, the grocery landscape in the United States is beginning to change and to resemble the European and Canadian landscapes. The number of American grocery consolidations is increasing and Wal-Mart, the huge American national chain, is ranked the fourth largest food retailer on Supermarket News's top 75 list in 1996. According to Harvey, M., Rothe,

J. T. and Lucas, L. A., one factor that might influence the growth of American private labels is the increased level of European investment in the United States. Several European retailers have been investing in American chains such as Ahold, N.V. of the Netherlands owning ninety percent of First National Supermarkets, Tengelmann of Germany owning fifty three percent of AtP, Delhaize of Belgium owning fifty percent of Food Lion, and J. Sainsburg controlling Shaws.

PROPITIOUS LANDSCAPE

According to Murray, R. (1999), the United States is the most important market for private label in terms of sales volume, but the country is ranked between the fifth and the eighth place in the world regarding global share. According to Kahn and McAlister (1997), the high-quality private label was introduced during the 1980's in response to the new landscape in the United States. The new landscape included four important characteristics. First of all, consumers were getting harder to reach since they were becoming more diverse. Second, advertising media was becoming more expensive and less effective due to media fragmentation. Third, brands were becoming less and less different and, finally, retailers and wholesalers were consolidating and becoming bigger and more sophisticated.

1. Consumers Becoming More Diverse

In 1980, the minority population including African Americans, Hispanic Americans, and Asian Americans represented nineteen percent of the total population in the United States and this number increased to twenty seven percent in 1997. In addition, consumers have been getting increasingly busy, without time to watch television and pay attention to advertising anymore. Women, who used to work in the house and thus probably had time to watch television, have been working outside the house lately. According to the Bureau of Labor Statistics, in 1950, only twenty percent of households received dual income (husband and wife) while sixty five percent received traditional income (husband-only). In 1993, forty five percent of households were receiving dual income (husband and wife) while only fifteen percent were receiving traditional income (husband).

2. Advertising More Expensive and Less Effective

In the past, the most important challenge for private labels in the United States was the television advertising in which national brands had the opportunity to create and build loyalty and to communicate emotions and promises to the consumers. However, according to a Point of Purchase Institute survey, there has been a decline of brand loyalty lately and advertising is becoming more and more expensive and less and less effective. In the 1960's, eighty percent of consumers went to supermarkets in order to purchase specific brands. Today, over sixty six percent of all purchase decisions are only made at the point of purchase.

In 1980, a household had access to an average number of ten television channels. This number jumped to sixty in 1997 and tends to increase even more. The number of magazines' titles jumped from 1,450 in 1980 to 2,135 in 1990 and the number of radio stations jumped from 7,871 in 1980 to 9,470 in 1990. In addition to this huge media fragmentation, consumers are no longer trusting advertising. They are becoming more skeptical in brand selection and in the marketing game and they are less interested in traditional signs of success such as "new", improved" and "latest" and much more interest in higher quality and lower price.

The excess of advertising clutter is making it harder for any brand to differentiate its message through a creative way. Regarding media viewing habits, the percent of VCR penetration per household was only two percent in 1980 and jumped to eighty three percent in 1997 and the penetration of remote control TV per household was twenty nine percent in 1985 and increased to ninety seven percent in 1997. It is getting harder for brands to appeal to a broad audience with one message and one product as well as to build brand awareness and brand equity.

3. Less Differentiation Among Brands

According to the Marketing Intelligence Service, Producstan, among the total number of items launched to the market lately, the number of truly new products is declining. The majority of the new launches represents only line extension such as a different flavor, size or color. In addition to that, the brands are becoming more and more equal and according to Kahn and McAlister (1997), the parity is getting worst since manufacturers are strongly offering price reductions through the use of coupons. Coupons, rebates and other price reductions instigate consumers to try different products, diminishing brand loyalty among them.

4. Grocery Consolidation

According to Blumenthal, I. (1998), the president of an Atlanta-based business development firm whose clients are Coca Cola, Nestle, and Exxon, the grocery consolidation is not a new phenomenon, but it has been increasing dramatically lately. Several mergers, acquisitions, joint ventures, and alliances have been taking place in the retail industry including supermarkets, grocery stores, super-stores and so on, not only in America but all over the world. The money is becoming concentrated in fewer and bigger retail chains.

According to the Food Institute, the number of consolidations grew forty percent from 1997 to 1998. Some examples of this trend since the beginning of 1996 are Vons Cos.' acquisition by Safeway, Giant Food's acquisition by Ahold USA, Nob Hill Foods' acquisition by Raley's, Seessel's acquisition by Albertson's, Fresh Fields' acquisition by Whole Foods, Alfafa's acquisition by Wild Oats and Albertson's merger with American Stores.

Blumenthal (1998) states that a consolidation, when well managed, may bring value, efficiency and growth to several chains. Consolidation also allows competitiveness and opportunities since the chains can count on partnerships and alliances to increase skills of technology, research, marketing information about consumers and, thus, better customer satisfaction. Groceries are becoming bigger, more efficient with greater value-added and they are successfully selling their branding because they have more presence and can reach more and more consumers. Therefore, their respective private labels tend to follow this path. Private labels are stronger, more present, and more reachable. With the consolidation, private labels represent an excellent opportunity for retailers due to the gap between the cost of raw materials and the price of national brands. Since the product's focus has switched to the consumer (Raphel, M., 1999), several grocery chains want to take control of their offers and thus provide private labels, which means exclusivity and allows better margins than national brands.

According to Harvey, M. Rothe, J. T. & Lucas, L. A., retailers are using a cross-brand cannibalization strategy, which means selling private labels that resemble national brands regarding brand names and packaging' attributes such as colors, sizes and formats, without infringing trademarks. Retailers keep selling nationally branded products but instigate consumers to switch to their private labels and this cross-brand cannibalization brings positive consequences for the retailers such as more independence from the national brands and a possibility for branding the retailer establishment.

SPECIFIC CATEGORIES OF PRIVATE LABELS

Private labels have higher unit share than national brands in seventy seven of two hundred and fifty product categories and they are second or third in one hundred products of those categories. In 1998, for example, private labels increased almost thirteen percent in unit sales in drug store chains, according to Murray, R. (1999).

The cigarette category was the most significant success story illustrating the growth of private labels. While the price of a Marlboro's pack was US$ 2 in 1993, the price of a cigarette-private label's pack was US$ 69 cents. The cigarette private label category increased its market share from eleven percent in 1988 to over forty percent in 1993. According to Kahn and McAlister (1997), Phillip Morris decided to cut the price of Marlboro by forty percent on April 2, 1993, which resulted in a US$ 13.4 billion fall in stock prices.

Not only Phillip Morris, but also several traditional manufacturers such as Procter & Gamble, Coca-Cola, PepsiCo, Quaker Oaks and Gillette have been menaced by private labels and, therefore, had to cut their prices. The total loss of the market value due to national brands' price reduction was US$ 47.5 billion. By the end of 1993, most of the categories that were traditionally dominated by national brands, began to be dominated by private labels. The market share of private labels has been increasing rapidly as illustrated by the following examples: the soft drink category increased fifteen percent, the cold cereal category increased twenty-seven percent, the diapers increased eighteen percent, the cookies increased twenty-seven percent and the cigarettes increased fifty-six percent.

Regarding the clothing category, fifty-three percent of consumers think private labels have the same quality as national brands. Regarding the price, forty-seven percent still consider private labels clothing to be a good deal while forty six percent believe private label clothing costs the same as national brands clothing and twenty three percent consider private labels clothing even more expensive than national brands clothing (Setlow, C., 1998). Therefore, consumers are provided with a large selection of options in the clothing category including national brands and private labels. On the other hand, retailers, when carrying private label clothing and national brand clothing, are provided with several opportunities to attract different consumers.

Regarding the cosmetics category, there still is a predominance of national brands. According to Setlow, C. (1998), sixty seven percent of cosmetic consumers buy national brands. Other categories that still have a predominance of national brands regarding consumer preferences are athletic shoes, men's jeans, women's jeans, coffee, and tea bags (Setlow, C. 1998). Those categories seem to deal with a greater level of loyalty by the consumers regarding the brands or private labels for those categories are not providing high enough quality products so far.

Regarding the cold cereal category, the average price of a national brand was US$ 5 a box while the private label's price was US$ 3.5 a box. According to Murray, R. (1999), consumers saved more than US$ 230 million just buying private labels of cold cereal. The market share of the private label cereal category increased from five percent in 1990 to eight percent in 1995. The national cereal brands' manufacturers started to fight against private labels. Post, a business unit of Phillip Morris company's Kraft division, cut cereal prices by twenty percent. Kellogg's also cut the price by nineteen percent, and then General Mills and Quaker Oats also reacted, cutting their prices.

The fastest growing private labels categories of products are weight loss/protein supplement, rice and popcorn cakes, sugar substitutes and Mexican sauces. According to a McKinsey study of private labels in Europe, the penetration is highest for those categories that are technologically less sophisticated, with little product innovation and in which the price difference between private labels and national brands is high.

According to Quelch, J. A. and Harding, D. (1996), there are five categories of factors that drive private-label market shares. The first category is related to product characteristics. The share will depend on if the product is an inexpensive, easy, low-risk purchase for the consumer, if it is easy to make from commodities' ingredients and if it is perishable, thereby favoring local suppliers. It will also depend on if the product category sales are large and growing, so private labels can more easily garner sufficient volume to be profitable and if the category is dominated by a few national-brand manufacturers, so retailers promote private labels to reduce dependency on them.

The second group of factors, according to Quelch, J. and Harding, D. (1996), is related to new-product activity. These factors include if national brands are offered in few varieties, enabling a private label with a narrow line to represent a clear alternative to the consumer and if national-brand new-product introductions are infrequent or easy to copy. It also includes if consumers can easily make side-by-side comparisons of national brands and private labels.

Regarding the third group of factors, the share will depend on if the private-label goods have been available to consumers for many years, if the distribution is well-developed and if the variability in quality is low. In addition to that, if the quality in comparison with national brands is high and improving and if consumers have confidence in their ability to make comparisons about quality.

Quelch, J. and Harding, D. (1996)'s fourth group includes price and promotions factors. If the retail gross margins in the product category are relatively high, if the price gaps between national brands and private labels are wide, and if national-brand expenditures on price promotions as a percentage of sales are high, raising price sensitivity and encouraging consumers to switch brands. Also, if the credibility of national-brand prices is low because of frequent and deep price promotions and national-brand expenditures on advertising as a percentage of sales are low.

Finally, the fifth group includes retailer characteristics; if the retailer is part of a stable oligopoly and therefore sells national brands at relatively high prices and if the retailer has the size and resources to invest in high-quality private-label development.

PRIVATE LABELS AS REAL BRANDS

Suzette, H. (1999) in her article "The branding of private labels" and Thompson, S. (1999) in her article "The new private enterprise" say that the difference between brand and private labels has been narrowing lately. Private labels are being treated as real brands. Due to the consolidation of the grocery channels, retailers are becoming more and more sophisticated. Consequently, their private labels are improving in quality, consistency and overall image. Retailers are beginning to develop their own promotions for their private labels and national manufacturers are facing a hard time to gain and sustain shelve space and special displays. Therefore, the power has been shifting to the retail side.

Since private labels are becoming closer to real brands, they have to act like real brands. However, acting like real brands is not an easy task and private labels face a serious problem. If they are successful, they are a great value for the retailers. On the other hand, if one category of private label faces a bad experience, it could spread to other categories or to the store as a whole. Consumers can get Kellogg's cold cereal at any store, but they cannot get private labels' cold cereal brands anywhere but at the respective store. Therefore, according to Thompson, S. (1999), retailers have to work harder, offering quality and innovation and allocating a huge amount of time and resources to package development.

Several retailers are developing a brand and product management department to manage private labels as real brands. H-E-B, a channel from San Antonio, Texas, built its department structure for managing private labels inspired by the benchmark Sainbury's model for retailer branding, in which fifty percent of the share was for their own label. H-E-B's structure is similar to any national manufacturer, including brand development managers, quality assurance technologies, sensory department, label design studio, marketing & promotional tools, market research, media positioning and direct mail marketing.

Due to this brand-department, H-E-B can keep leveraging its own brands, offering lower prices, building loyalty, and increasing profitability. H-E-B is filling a very interesting gap, which is represented by the enormous change regarding private labels prior to 1992, when there were only traditional private labels. H-E-B's most important current challenge is related to consumer perception of store brands products. H-E-B wants to make consumers perceive the differences between HEB brand and Hill country Fare. H-E-B has a different positioning for each brand such as Hill Country Fare for the "price-conscious-consumer" and H-E-B brand for the "quality-standard-consumer."

Since the distance between private labels and national brands is narrowing and private labels have been treated as real brands, national brands must begin to approach the market through a different perspective. Before suggesting some advice for national brands, it is very important to understand their universe and several concepts related to the issue of branding such as loyalty, equity, identity, personality and so on.

Part 2

BRANDING – BUILDING BRANDS

A brand, according to Raphel, M. (1999), is "something that exists in the minds and actions of the customer and the relationship between the customer and a product or item" (pp.29). Among the most powerful US brands are Coca Cola, Campbell's, Disney, Pepsi Cola, Kodak, NBC, Black & Decker, Kellogg's, McDonald's, Hershey's, Levi Strauss, General Electric, Sears Roebuck, Hallmark and Johnson & Johnson (Donahue, D. M., 1995).

Quelch and Harding (1996) say that those strongest national brands built themselves over several years developing advertising and delivering quality. During those years, there has been almost no change in the ranking of the top 50 brands. According to an Equitrend's consumer survey, forty of the top fifty brands were the same in 1993 and in 1991. According to a survey developed by DDB Needham in 1994, sixty percent of consumers still prefer the comfort, security, and value of a national brand to a private label. This percentage is much lower than in the 1970s, however, it remained constant during the last decade.

THE HISTORY OF BRANDING

The brand as a concept appeared for the first time in the medieval times when a tradesman put his unique stamp on products such as gold, silver, pewter and clothes (Donahue, M. D, 1995) in order to attribute value to them. The stamp became a trademark since everyone knew those products belonged to that particular tradesman. However, it was very hard to physically print the stamp in some products such as beers and whiskies. Therefore, the tradesman had to start printing the stamp into the bottles and barrels, but making sure that the product inside the recipient was authentic and therefore transmitted the same message to the consumers.

Germany, Portugal and Holland were the world's three first global marketers countries, even before America was discovered (Donahue, M. D.). Those countries sometimes could not ship the perishable product to other parts of the world but they were able to ship formulas, techniques and skills to reproduce products in other countries. Nowadays, a trademarked product is associated with several other issues such as a combination of numbers, letters, arches and symbols and those issues are not simply "cosmetic enhancements" (Donahue, M. D, 1995. 13), but emotions and promises.

THE CONCEPT OF BRAND

A brand is a combination of tangible and intangible characteristics. "It is the totality of the thoughts, feelings, associations and expectations a prospect or customer experiences when he or she is exposed to the company's name, trademarks, labels, product or the designs and symbols representing them" (Donahue, M. D., 1995, 14). For example, Honda means quality and reliability in the United States and Volvo means security.

According to Donahue, M. D. (1995) a brand would succeed if it transmits "one consistent and evocative message about one specific demonstrable quality that differentiates itself from the competition" (p. 21). The brand must avoid being a set of meaningless and undifferentiated products fighting for share of voice, but rather compete to share of mind, allocating energy to a single, unique and important message.

BRANDS AND PERCEIVED QUALITY

Besides filling a specific promise, the three most important and valuable attributes related to brand building are trustworthiness, relevance and distinction and those attributes are related to the perceived quality of that brand. A brand needs to achieve a level of quality and this takes much more than simply developing a quality product. The brand has to create a quality brand relationship, which according to Donhaue, M. D. (1995) means a quality product marketed in a quality way. Quality is not only related to engineering or technology of the product, but also to every small aspect related to the brand. Consumers should believe that the brand would deliver the "highest distinctive expectation that is relevant to the markets in which the brand is competing"(Donhaue, p.23).

In a study conducted by Josh McQueen of Leo Burnett agency in 1993, over one hundred consumers were questioned on seventy-four of their major brands. According to the survey, high scores for quality did not relate in any way to the score for high value. However, there was a huge correlation between quality and value regarding the combination of quality, relevance and distinction averaged as a group and then merged with the scores on price.

According to Donahue M. D. (1995), the study conducted by Josh McQueen shows that every brand has a price so high at which it becomes too expensive and a price so low that consumer would doubt the brand's equity. Therefore, there is a range of acceptable prices and different profiles of consumers will attribute different weights between quality and price. Consumers are usually not that concerned if the product is good or cheap, but rather about the cost/ benefit relations, which means whether or not the product benefits are worth the money to spent.

CONSUMER SATISFACTION AND BRANDING

While consumer satisfaction is a crucial element for business survival, it is not enough for branding and for building a loyal relationship between the consumer and the brand. According to the Senior Vice President of the American Association of Advertising Agencies in his presentation *"Translating Vision into a Meaningful Identity: Brand Loyalty Marketing"*, fifty percent of the consumers who are completely satisfied with a specific product do not repurchase it. Moreover, repeat behavior is not the same as loyal behavior. Besides consumer satisfaction, brands must consider consumer delight as an efficient strategy in order to create and sustain a loyal and strong relationship with its consumers.

BRAND IDENTITY

Within a landscape of media cluster and information overload, brand leadership requires strong brand identity building, which is what the brand should stand for. According to Aaker & Joachimsthole (1999), clarity and enthusiasm about the association the brand aspires to develop is essential to build brand identity. Several companies have several different ways to expose their brands' identities. Unilever has a very detailed manual that tells everything about the Lipton Tea brand, for example, such as what does Lipton Tea stand for? What are the timeless elements of that brand? What brand-building programs are off target, and so on. Nestle uses workshops, Hewlett-Packard uses newsletters, Volvo uses books and catalogues and The Limited uses video to communicate and educate about issues of brands identity.

BRAND EQUITY

Brands have always been the most significant resource that the majority of the companies have among several things and, different from patents and copyrights, brands are the only forms of intellectual property that never expire. Donhahue (1995) says "founders die, factories burn down, machinery wears out, inventories get depleted, technology becomes obsolete." However, brands are expected to last forever.

When talking about brand equity, it is very important to talk about measurement. During the 1990s, Pepsi launched an efficient system to measure brand equity called "market-place P&L". This measurement tracked the results of blind taste tests, the extent of a product's distribution and results of customer opinion surveys about the brand. When the system was launched, its use was optional and Pepsi brand managers were recommended to use it. However, the company realized the value of the measurement system and in 1998, the CEO Roger Enrico made the system mandatory since it was improving the brand building efforts (Aaker, D. A. & Joachimsthole, E., 1999)

BRAND AND CONSUMER: A STRONG RELATIONSHIP

Understanding the dynamic of a brand and building a strong relationship between the brand and the consumer are two tough processes that require time and patience. It is necessary to understand the universe of the consumer and to conduct several researches and focus groups in order to build a strong brand. The relationship between the brand and the consumer has to be built under trust and this trust would make consumers loyal to the brand.

Every brand manager's goal is to create a strong relationship based on trustfulness and loyalty between the brand and the consumer. Susan Fournier, a Harvard's specialist of "brand-as-relationship" concept says that there are seven dimensions that explain how an ideal relationship between the brand and the consumer should be.

The first dimension is related to behavioral independence and approaches feelings such as "this brand plays an important role in my life" or "I feel like something's missing when I haven't used the brand in a while". The second dimension according to Fournier is related to personal commitment and some of the feelings are "I feel very loyal to this brand" or "I will stay with this brand through good times and bad times". The third dimension is related to love and passion and as the specialist points out, approaches ideas such as "no other brand can quite take the place of this brand" or "I would be very upset if I could not find this brand". The fourth dimension is related to nostalgic connection and some of the feelings are "this brand reminds me of things I've done or places I've been." or "this brand will always remind me of a particular phase of my life. The fifth dimension is related to self-concept connection and approaches ideas such as "the brand's and my self image are similar" and the brand reminds me of who I am". The sixth dimension according to Fournier is related to intimacy and some of the feelings are "I know a lot about this brand" and "I know a lot about the company that makes this brand". Finally, the seventh dimension is related to partner of quality and approaches ideas such as "I know this brand really appreciates me" and "this brand treats me like a valued customer". Susan Fournier says that while the first three dimensions are related to brand loyalty, the other four are related to different kinds of relationships.

BRAND PERSONALITY

For every brand's behavior, there is usually a respective personality trait. According to Aaker (1996) in his book *"Building Strong Brands"*, if the brand usually changes its positioning, its product's attributes, its packaging or its advertising often, consumers may consider the brand flighty and schizophrenic. In case the brand provides deals and coupons frequently, consumers may consider the brand cheap and uncultured. Aaker continues that if the brand advertises a lot, consumers may consider the brand very popular and outgoing. In case the brand provides strong customer service, easy-to-use package and other attributes, the brand may be perceived as approachable. If the brand provides high price, exclusive distribution and advertises in upscale magazines, consumers may perceive it as snobbish and sophisticated. If the brand uses a friendly advertising, consumers may perceive it as friendly and if a brand is associated with cultural events, it may be perceived as culturally aware.

Among some examples, Aaker mentions Apple Macintosh. Since it is an easy-to-use and intuitive computer that even greets its user, the brand is always perceived as friendly, unpretentious, irreverent and willing to go against the grain. Betty Crocker, according to him, is perceived as traditional, related to small-town and to all-American mother who cares about cooking and about her family. The reason for this perception is the familiar symbol of the Betty Crocker face that provides a strong visual image. Several consumers consider that Betty Crocker reminds them of childhood memories.

Nike is, according to Aaker, an aspirational brand. Due to the presence of Michael Jordan, Andre Agassi, Bo Jackson and several other sport-related personalities, wearing Nike represents what the users aspire to be like rather than their current self-image and the brand is perceived as spirited, stylish, determined to excel and into health and fitness. Regarding the imported vodka category, Aaker mentions Stolichnaya and Absolut, the two brands that have been competing for several years. The brands are similar in some points like high quality, purity and image, but they have completely different brand perception among the consumers. Stolichnaya is perceived as experienced, self-assured, and successful in a traditional career such as law or banking while Absolut is perceived as young, fashion, related to arts and trendy.

BRAND LOYALTY

Regarding loyalty, there is not a totally loyal consumer but rather several levels of loyalty. Measuring loyalty, differently from measuring market share, is a very hard task. However, measuring loyalty is very needed since it has a huge impact in the brand's profitability. There are several different ways to measure brand loyalty. Kathleen MacDonnell, President of Campbell's frozen food division has an interesting ranking including four categories: 1. Avoid, 2. Borderline, 3. Profitable and 4. Most profitable.

According to MacDonnell, since customers are not equal regarding to their level of loyalty, product research or communication should not consider them equally. In addition to that, she believes that products should be target to the taste of the most loyal segments of the market, which are the most profitable, and not to the average consumer. Finally, the interests and experiences of the loyal segments of the consumer base should determine the brand's marketing and media spending as well as any other important decision related to the brand and not the entire population of potential buyers.

David Aaker (1991) in his book *"Managing Brand Equity"* offers several levels to measure brand loyalty and those levels may be positioned as if they were in a pyramid. The most inferior level of the pyramid includes the non-loyal consumer, totally indifferent about the brand. For this consumer, each brand is perceived as being reasonable and the name of the brand has very low importance in his buying decision. He will prefer any other competitor brand that is available in the store. This kind of consumer is usually very sensitive to the price of the product.

The second level of the pyramid includes consumers who are satisfied with the product or at least non-unsatisfied. There is no dissatisfaction that would instigate this consumer to change to other brand. This segment of consumers is not looking for other alternatives but can easily be convinced by the competition to try other products.

The third level according to Aaker approaches those consumers who are also satisfied and are afraid about changing to another brand due to possible switching costs associated with the change such as time, money or performance. Those consumers sometimes do not want to take the risk of the substitute brand having lower quality than the current brand. In order to attract those consumers, competition needs to find ways to eliminate or at least reduce those switching costs by offering compensation benefits.

In the fourth group of the pyramid there are the consumers who really like the brand. They usually like a symbol, a set of experiences with usage, or a high quality perceived. This is a general feeling and is not related to one specific attribute of the brand. There is an emotional friendship relation in this level between the brand and the consumer.

Aaker says that the higher level of the pyramid refers to committed consumers. They are proud of being brand pioneers or frequent users. The brand is not only important because of its function but also because it is an expression about them. Those consumers are extremely loyal to the brand and they trust the brand so that they will recommend the brand to other people. The value of this group of consumers is not only related to the individual level but to their ability to promote the brand through word-of-mouth and to attract consumers in the other levels of the pyramid. Aaker, D. (1991) provides examples of these consumers such as a Harley Davidson user who has the symbol of the brand as a tattoo or a Macintosh user who attends the company's presentations and makes every possible thing to convince a friend not to buy other brand of computers.

Those five levels of loyalty will not always appear in a plain and simple manner. Sometimes, there would be consumers who mix those five levels such as consumers who are not satisfied with a specific brand but are concerned anyway about the cost associated with switching to other brands. However, those five levels provide a solid basis for analysis regarding to the variety of forms of loyalty and how they impact the brand equity.

In order to measure the brand loyalty, Aaker, D. (1991) suggests brands' manufacturers to analyze issues related to the real purchasing patterns of consumers such as the re-purchase index, the purchase percentage, and the number of brands purchased. The brand loyalty can vary a lot among consumers, depending on the product category's nature and on the number of competitors. Although very objectives, the purchasing patterns behaviors have limitations. They can be inconvenient and expensive to be achieved and they only provide a limited diagnosis about the future. In addition to that, its usage may bias those consumers who really changed brands. Another important measurement for brand loyalty, according to Aaker is by measuring consumer satisfaction and dissatisfaction. It is important to know if consumers are facing problems with the brands and why they are switching brands.

UNDERSTANDING BRAND LOYALTY – CRUCIAL FOR BRANDS

Brand loyalty has been considered the key for national brands to achieve sustainable and profitable growth for several years. Several companies target a huge amount of promotional efforts to non-loyal consumers in order to convince them to purchase the product. Besides hurting the profitability of the company, this does not seem to be the most efficient strategy.

A Campbell's study about response to promotion showed that sixty five percent of the brand users buying fifty one percent of the volume returned just thirty eight cents on Campbell's marketing and media investment. However, only four percent of the buyers doing only fifteen percent of the volume returned nearly ten times that amount. The reason for that is that loyal consumers who bought more of the product did not wait for deals but rather bought the product when they wanted it, usually paying a higher price. Loyal consumers did not use deals to cut costs even with the availability of lower prices.

Therefore, the president of Campbell's frozen food division concluded that she was wasting her marketing budget including trade promotions and incentives with her least loyal and therefore least profitable segment of consumers. She was wasting US$20 million out of US$29 million marketing budget, representing ninety five percent of advertising wasted, sixty three percent of trade promotion wasted and sixty percent of total marketing dollars wasted.

What happened with Campbell is typical. Several important national brands' manufacturers make the same mistakes. They tend to offer several deals and promotions to the disloyal shoppers such as trade allowances, price reductions, refunds, gifts, sweepstakes and coupons. Those deals are volume-building activities that punish the best and loyal consumers as well as hurt the companies' profitability and do not create loyalty like brand-building activities such as demonstrations, seminars, shows, effective service material (brochures, video, etc.), public relations, advertising, direct marketing and promotions that extend positioning.

According to Fred Reichheld (1993) from Bain & Company in his article published at the ***Harvard Business Review,*** the longer a brand keeps a customer, the deeper his loyalty. And the deeper his loyalty, the higher the brand's profit. He also says that loyal shoppers are not rented but rather owned and they do not wait until their favorite products are on sale to buy them because they always believe in the product's value regardless the discount-price.

On the other hand, shoppers with little or no brand loyalty are expected to be much more price-sensitive and they would buy whatever acceptable product offers the best price, which means they will accept the deal regardless of which brand has offered it.

LOYALTY AS A STRATEGIC ISSUE

The brand loyalty is the most valuable and strategic issue a national brand can use in order to compete against other national brands. Loyalty to the brand provides time, an advantage gap for the national brand to react against actions taken by other national brands (Aaker, D., 1991). If a competitor develops and launches a new product, the brand loyalty will allow the necessary time for the brand to take same precautions in order to neutralize the performance of the new competitor's launch.

For example, in a high-tech category, consumers can be attracted by competition new and technologically superior launch if there is low brand loyalty by consumers within that brand's category. On the other hand, loyal and satisfied consumers are not looking for other products and therefore may not become aware about the competitor's new launch. Even when consumers are exposed to the launch, they will not be motivated to change to the competitor's product because of their great loyalty for the current brand.

PRIVATE LABELS AS COMPETITORS

However, when the competition includes private label and not only national brands, the loyalty may no longer be a strategic edge. Private labels usually offer much lower prices and if consumers are more price-sensitive than loyal to brands, they tend to change their minds and purchase private labels instead of national brands. The growth of private labels is therefore changing the entire branding approach. Switching brands does not require the same amount of efforts and energy as used to be before the success of private labels. Private labels can simply offer the same quality of products at a lower price and thus conquer price-sensitive or non-loyal consumers.

Some rules of thumb such as "stay closer to the consumer", "treat the consumer well", "care about consumer satisfaction", "create switching costs" and "offer something extra", may no longer work when brands are also competing against private labels for a price-sensitive consumer. It is necessary that national brand's manufacturers approach an entire new branding concept that begins analyzing the price-sensitivity of the consumer, his level of loyalty and so on.

Part III

NEW BRANDING APPROACH

Private labels have been succeeding lately and they represent a serious challenge and menace for traditional national brands. According to Quelch, J. A. and Harding, D. (1996) in their article "Brands Versus Private Labels: Fighting to Win", private labels represent a serious threat for national brands manufacturers regardless of economical conditions.

Therefore, national brands must rethink several issues related to the way they approach the market in order to learn how to share the shelves with private labels and compete against them in sales. National brands must consider some important marketing strategies which although will depend a lot on each category, some basic and common issues apply to all of them:

1. Knowledge about Consumers

National brands must understand, more than ever, the consumers' universe, their motivations, desires and shopper habits in order to comprehend which issues are important for them while purchasing the respective category and which issues are not that relevant. Depending on the product category, consumers may value different attributes such as quality, variety, price, and so on and understanding those attributes would make national brands manufacturers ahead to take decisions.

2. Knowledge about Loyalty

It is also recommended for national brands to understand the level of loyalty that exists in its respective product category. Since private labels are more successful when there is low loyalty in the category, national brands can expect stronger private labels' competition within those product categories with lower brand loyalty.

3. Knowledge about Price Sensitivity

It is recommended for national brands to understand issues related to price sensitivity in each category. In order to understand consumers' price sensitivity, it is necessary to analyze the brand's economic value. Nagle, T. T. & Holden, R. K. (1995) provide some factors that affects consumers' price sensitivity as well as several techniques to analyze each of them.

Perceived substitutes effect is related to the number of alternatives that consumers are aware of when making a purchase decision and national brands' manufacturers can visit or call some distributors and retailers to find out information about competition's brands and prices.

Another attribute is related to unique value effect and addresses if the brand has unique attributes that differentiate itself from competition' brands and which attributes do consumers value when making a purchase. In order to find information about unique value of the brand, national brands' manufacturers can use observation and formal researches such as conjoint analyses with consumers. The hard task is not to identify those values but rather to place a value to them.

The third factor is the switching cost effect and is related to the monetary and psychological investment a consumer has already made and would need to make again if he switched to another brand. Information regarding this effect can be obtained through formal or informal surveys with consumers.

Price-quality is another effect and is related to the quality of the brand perceived being worth the price. Conducting simple surveys is not always efficient since consumers do not tend to answer those questions easily. Brand manufacturers should rely on judgment based on the comparison of similar brands' categories or count on experimental research to measure price's value according to the quality offered.

According to Nagle, T. T. & Holden, R. K. (1995), another factor that affects price sensitivity is the expenditure effect and is related to the relevance of the brand's price for the consumer's income. National brands' manufacturers can obtain this information through government agencies, trade associations, and private companies that collect data on consumers' incomes. Manufacturers can also conduct their own direct mail or telephone survey to acquire those data.

Another factor is the inventory effect and is related to if consumers hold inventory of the product. National brands' manufacturers can obtain information about consumer's inventory through survey research and past buyer behavior.

When consumers are sensitive to prices, they tend to buy more private labels' brands. Price sensitive consumers would not mind switching brands in order to achieve the cheapest product, which is probably the private label. Combining the fact that private labels are also providing quality and other attributes besides the lower price, national brands are facing serious challenges.

However, private labels shoppers are neither necessarily price-sensitive nor promotion-oriented consumers. According to a study measuring consumers' attitudes toward private label brands, despite a positive relationship between the private label attitude and promotions, consumers who purchased more private label products than national brands, purchased fewer products on sale or using coupons. (Burton, S., Lichtenstein, D. R., Netemeyer, R.G. & Garretson, J. A, 1998).

4. Knowledge about Shopping Behavior

Although the economy is going well, as Bansal, M. (1998) points out, consumers are getting savvy in their shopping habits and skeptical about some brands. Therefore, it is very recommended for national brands' manufacturers to research consumer shopping behavior. McLuhan, R. (1999) suggests five different methods that manufacturers can use to analyze consumer's shopping behavior.

Interviews and focus groups are traditional methods in use since the early 1980s. There is another traditional method called "accompanied shop" in which the researcher walks around the store with the consumer. Traditional methods are easy to proceed but provide very subjective information.

The second method is video surveillance, consisting by video cameras that record consumer's shopping behavior. The cameras are usually fixed in a specific area of the retailer establishment or sometimes controlled by a cameraman. A psychologist needs to analyze the tape using benchmarks for the specific category. Although costly, this is a very efficient method.

The third method according to McLuhan, R. (1999) approaches proximity detectors. Those miniature infra-red sensors, inserted in the point of purchase stand, record the number of consumers who passes in a specific area of the store, the number of consumers who stop to look at a specific product and the time consumers spend looking at the product. According to McLuhan, this method is easy to manage, relatively cheap and is able to provide large samples.

The fourth method is eye mark recorder. For this method, consumers have to use a head-band with elastic and equipped with a tiny micro camera that sees everything that consumers are seeing. An infrared beam records consumer's eye movements, identifying what they are looking at and for how long. This method requires consumer's participation but is very useful to identify the impact of stand design.

Finally, the fifth method is virtual reality, which is a new method launched by ID Magasin. The issue of this method is to create a fictitious retail environment in order to test the reactions of consumers. Although this method is currently expensive, it is expected to become cheaper as the technology develops further (McLuhan, R., 1999).

5. Knowledge about Competition

Besides knowing who the other national brands' competitors are, national brands' manufacturers must consider private labels as real competitors and also be aware about them. National brands need to stop considering other national brands as its real competition. The growth of premium private labels should be considered a dangerous competitor. They start stealing market share from weak national brands and this opens the door to the entire category. National brands should allocate time, money and energy to develop marketing actions to compete against private label.

According to Quelch and Harding, even legal actions can be taken against private labels sometimes since they copy packaging designs, formats and colors of national brands or they use proprietary technology in the manufacture of private labels. Some private labels steal the promise of a national brand while copying the national brand's packaging. They copy several packaging' attributes such as colors, formats, size and typography in order to communicate the same promise while they are side by side on the shelves and this can be considered intellectual property's crime and needs to be protected in the courtroom or in the marketplace.

It is very important to understand private labels' strengths and weaknesses as well as their current market share and future goals in order to take efficient decisions and reactions based on this information.

6. Being Innovative and Creative

Innovation and Creativity are two strategic issues that national brands' manufacturers should use against private labels. Besides creating new products and services, national brands' corporations should find creative ways to quickly manufacture and distribute them to the market in order for them to be immediately available for consumers.

National brands' manufacturers need to be creative in the implementation of the process of designing, engineering, building, testing, promoting, and distributing the product. National brands' manufacturers have the challenge to motivate creativity in order to enhance profits.

There are many ways national brands' manufacturers can use creativity to compete against private labels such as to create cheaper alternatives of distribution channels, suppliers, or packages. De Bono (1992) notes that: In practice, cost-cutting requires a great deal more creativity than most people imagine. It is not just a simple matter of cost-benefit analysis. It is not only a matter of choosing to give up the benefit if it does not justify the cost. It is also a matter of finding ways to achieve the same benefit at less cost (p. 22).

An interesting case happened in the cereal market. According to Leonhardt (1998), the demand for cereals decreased for three main reasons. First, private label cereal products were succeeding due to their lower price and good quality. Second, prices of the products were very expensive because traditional cereal companies were facing high costs of package development. Also, breakfast habits of people were changing. Always busy with so many activities, consumers were preferring to eat something faster and more practical such as muffins and bagels for breakfast.

Big cereal companies faced a hard time because consumers were not willing to pay very much for nationally branded cereals. Kellogg's, the biggest company in this category, was losing market share for private labels because its products were considered very expensive. The reason was that Kellogg's mark-up was affected by the high cost of product packaging: cereal boxes. Quaker Oats Co., the fourth cereal market competitor, came up with an innovative idea. Being aware of the private labels' success and the decrease of the cereal demand due to the high price of the box packaging, this company found a creative solution to offer the product in a bag, instead of in the expensive box. In this way, prices and overhead were kept lower.

7. Knowledge about Point-of-Purchase

National brands' managers must visit stores and retailers in order to check the performance of their brands. Besides only managing the brand through the office of the company, brand managers should conduct or at least accompany sales activities for a while. Brand managers should consider trade-marketing activities in spite of only working inside the office during the entire day of work. It is very important to check the brands' position on the shelves and the packaging while they are in the point of purchase.

8. Use of Trade Marketing

Trade marketing, a package-good philosophy first developed in the United States in 1980, combines the functions and responsibilities of two different departments: marketing and sales. This philosophy focuses on the integration between the manufacturing and the distribution, like a strategic alliance in which the communication is supposed to flow in both ways: marketing to sales and sales to marketing.

Since manufacturers are beginning to realize that consumers are making the majority of the final purchasing decisions in the stores, the trade marketing is becoming important. National brands' manufacturers are thus beginning to allocate a huge amount of the marketing budget to promotional investment in the point of purchase, expecting to communicate with consumers in the exact moment of the purchase decision.

National brands' manufacturers have to use the trade-marketing philosophy to understand the retail needs, to analyze them and to develop a plan including promotional actions, offers, merchandising in order to convince and attract retailers and distributors to purchase and distribute their brands.

Since the market is becoming more and more competitive and sophisticated and consumers are more informed and exigent, retailers are also becoming very exigent, willing to respect their consumers' claims. Therefore, retailers are only putting on the shelves products requested by consumers, which have the best prices.

It is crucial for national manufacturers to bring their marketing department closer to the distribution channels. Since the performance of the brand varies a lot depending on the region of the country, the trade marketing can identify important differences among channels and sub-channels as well as relevant geographic differences. The trade marketing philosophy also allows national brands' manufacturers the identification of the needs for different strategies and programs for each retail channel.

9. Use of Strategic Advertising Agencies

When deciding which advertising agency to do business with, national brands' manufacturers should look for agencies that truly understand the phenomenon of private labels. The agencies should also understand the level of loyalty and price sensitivity that exist in the respective product category in order to provide strategic advertising.

According to Zimmerman, S. (1998), several retailers have been advertising their private brands in the media lately and their campaigns are creative and efficient. J.C. Penney, for example, switched its private label line Arizona jeans US$20 million account to DDB Needham (Cuneo, A. Z., 1999), which is developing a very efficient job. Therefore, besides succeeding in sales, private labels are also disputing share of voice through great advertising.

10. Knowledge about Budget Allocation

Another important consideration is the allocation of the marketing budget between advertising and promotions. If the allocation of the marketing budget has always been one of the most complex decisions within the marketing, it is extremely crucial nowadays.

As Ashley, S. R. (1998) points out, promotions and price reductions are important strategies in order for national brands' manufacturers to compete against private labels in stores. However, the consequences of those deals are very negative for the companies' profitability. Therefore, national brands must be careful not to exceed and transform promotion into a disease, a vicious and prejudice too much their margin since private labels have much lower development and production costs.

One of the toughest decision for national brands' manufacturers regarding to marketing budget is how much to advertise and how much to promote. This is usually a trade-off given the budget restriction.

According to Alex Biel of Ogilvy Research, among seven hundred and forty nine brands, those brands whose advertising represented less than twenty five percent of the marketing mix had returns before taxes of eighteen percent. When the majority of the marketing expenditures was allocated to advertising, the company's profits before taxes almost doubled. Therefore, allocating twenty four percent of the marketing budget to advertising and seventy six percent to promotion provides a return before tax of eighteen percent. While allocating forty four percent in advertising and fifty six percent in promotion provides a twenty seven percent of return before tax. Finally, allocating fifty percent in advertising and fifty percent in promotion provides return before tax of thirty percent.

According to Donahue, M. D. (1995), Procter & Gamble and Lever Brothers spent over five billion dollars a year in marketing. According to Bob Prentice, an executive who worked as senior marketer for both companies, brand building activities that include advertising influence sales about four years and enhance the effect of non-brand building activities such as promotions. On the other hand, non-brand-building activities such as promotions influence sales less that one year and reduce or cancel out the effect of brand building activities such as advertising.

He also believes that brand-building activities allow higher percent of investment to be equal to higher profit since a higher investment in advertising correlates to higher profits. According to Bob Prentice, the number is fifty percent of all funds while Alex Biel from Ogilvy Research believes the number is forty four percent. In addition to that, Prentice believes that even price-sensitive commodity products such as paper towels still need some brand building activities and support including advertising, about thirty to thirty five percent of all available marketing budget. The non-brand building activities including promotions, coupons and price reductions provide higher percent of investment to be equal profits in decline within two years. Bob Prentice's main responsibilities included monitoring the research and comparing that with their media expenditures. Therefore he believes advertising incentives promotions but promotions damage the credibility of advertising.

Advertising is an investment and like any other investment, its return can be measured precisely. Advertising has important functions in the long time. It can create awareness, especially for those loyal consumers limited to the category. It can also change attitude, influence the acceptance of the product as a viable choice, increase preference, get the brand onto the consideration set, get consumers into the store and lead to the sale experience. According to Donahue, M. D. (1995), attitudes predict behavior, behavior predicts attitudes and loyalty is built through the product experience, the service experience, the after-sale service experience, the customer relations experience and contacts that reinforce the sale. In order to build brand loyalty, it is very important to build positive perceptions in the quality brand experience, in the market leadership and in the market share.

11. Knowledge about Advertising

National brands should keep advertising. When strategically planned and produced, advertising is very efficient. National brands should learn when and where to advertise in order to achieve cost-benefit as well as to waste less money and to get more efficiency.

According to Ashley, S. R. (1998), the traditional formula of building brands and communicating the high quality of the product through advertising in order to solve a consumer need is still efficient in creating differentiation within a price-competitive landscape. Of course, it is very important to build brand loyalty for the product category in order to differentiate the brand when among private labels and advertising can do this task very well. However, with the fragmentation of the channels, the strong penetration of VCR and remote control, the changing in consumers' habits, the clutter and information overload and with the high cost of mass media, it is been very challenged to produce efficient advertising lately.

CONCLUSION

The successful growth of private labels is really a huge phenomenon. Private labels have been increasing in number, quality and consumer acceptance, several consumers are buying private label instead of national brands and retailers are likely to offer both private labels and national brands in order to attract different consumers to the stores. Therefore, national brands must begin to consider private labels as strong competitors and thus, learn how to coexist with private labels, sharing space in the retail environment. National brands' manufacturers must also approach branding issues through a totally new spectrum and use several strategies in order to fight against private labels and win the battle.

REFERENCES

1. *Aaker, D. A. (1996) "Building Strong Brands", New York.*

2. *Aaker, D. A. & Joachimsthole, E. (1999). "The Lure of Global Branding". _**Harvard Business Review.** (Nov-Dec).*

3. *Ashley, S. R. (1998). How to effectively compete against private-label brands. **Journal of Advertising Research.** 38(1): 75-82. Jan/Feb.*

4. *Bansal, M. (1998). "Wooing a skeptical consumer". **Brandweek** 39 (47): 20-22. Dec. 14.*

5. *Blumenthal, I. (1998). "Grocery Consolidation: Strength in Numbers?" **Brandweek.** 39(41): 30. Nov 2.*

6. *Burton, S., Lichtenstein, D. R., Netemeyer, R. G., G.Arretson, J. A. (1998). "A scale for measuring attitude toward private label products and an examination of its psychological and behavioral correlates". **Journal of the Academy of Marketing Science.** 26(4): 293-306. Fall.*

7. *Cuneo, A. Z. (1999). "Penney's switches private-label Arizona line to DDB Needham". **Advertising Age.** 70(6): 2 Feb 8.*

8. *Cuneo, A. Z. (1999). "Retailtainment". **Advertising Age.** 70(39 (The Next Century Supplement)): 68,74.*

9. Dauw, D.C. & Fredian, A.J. (1971). ***Creativity and Innovation in Organizations.*** *Dubuque, Iowa: Kendall/Hunt Publishing Company.*

10. De Bono, E. (1992). Sur/Petition. *New York: HarperCollins Publishers, Inc.*

11. Donahue, M. D. (1995). ***Translating Vision into a Meaningful Identity: Brand Loyalty Marketing.*** *Advertising Research Foundation.*

12. Dunne, D. & Narasimhan, C. (1999). "The new appeal of private labels". ***Harvard Business Review.*** *77(3): 41-52. May/Jun.*

13. Harrison, D. (1998). "Private label evolution". ***Frozen Food Age. (Private Label Store Brands Supplement):*** *4-6. Mar.*

14. Harvey, M., Rothe, J. T. & Lucas, L. A. (1998). "The "trade dress" controversy: A case of strategic cross-brand cannibalization". ***Journal of Marketing Theory & Practice.*** *6(2): 1-15. Spring.*

15. Kahn, B.E. and McAlister, L. (1997). ***"Grocery Revolution. The New Focus on the Consumer".*** *Addison-Wesley Educational Publishers, Inc.*

16. Leonhardt, D. (October 12, 1998). Cereal-box killers are on the loose. ***Business Week,*** *72-77.*

17. McLuhan, R. (1999). "Impulse measures for POP creativity". ***Marketing.*** *31. Jun 3.*

18. Nagle, T. T. & Holden, R. K. (1995). **"The Strategy and Tactics of Pricing".** Prentice-Hall, Inc. Englewood Cliffs, NJ.

19. Quelch, J. A. and Harding, D. (1996). "Brands Versus Private Labels: Fighting to Win". ***Harvard Business Review.*** *– January-February 1996.*

20. Radice, C. (1998). "Private label: The differentiation dilemma". ***Progressive Grocer.*** *77 (4): 93-97. Apr.*

21. Raphel, M. (1999). "Branded!" ***Direct Marketing.*** *62(3): 29-30. Jul.*

22. Setlow, C. (1998). "Store brands and national brands share space in the shopping cart". ***Discount Store News.*** *37(12): 17. Jun 22.*

23. Suzette, H (1999). "The branding of private labels". ***Apparel Industry Magazine.*** *60(6): 72-76. Jun.*

24. Thompson, S. (1999). "The new private enterprise". ***Brandweek.*** *40(18): 36-48. May 3.*

25. Zimmerman, S. (1998). "A rosy future". ***Progressive Grocer.*** *77(11): 45-52.*